I0018786

Table Of Contents

Chapter 1: Introduction

Why DIY Mobile Device Repair?

In today's fast-paced, technology-driven world, our mobile devices have become indispensable. Whether it's for communication, work, entertainment, or keeping in touch with family, our smartphones are always by our side. However, just like any other electronic device, they are prone to wear and tear. From cracked screens to battery issues, or charging problems, device breakdowns can be frustrating.

DIY Mobile Device Repair is a great option for individuals who want to save money, learn new skills, and avoid the hassle of sending their device to a repair shop. Performing repairs on your device can be incredibly satisfying. Plus, it allows you to keep your phone or tablet for longer, without having to invest in a new one. This book will teach you how to perform basic to advanced repairs on your mobile device.

This chapter will introduce you to the basics of mobile device repair and equip you with the tools, knowledge, and mindset to take on your repair projects.

Tools You Will Need

Before beginning any repair, having the right tools is essential. The tools listed below are commonly used in mobile device repairs, and they'll help ensure you can perform repairs safely and effectively.

1. **Precision Screwdrivers**
   Mobile devices often use very small screws, which require specialized precision screwdrivers. Common screw types include:
   - **Pentalobe**: Apple devices typically use Pentalobe screws.
   - **Torx**: Often used for more general devices.
   - **Phillips**: Standard cross-head screwdrivers.
2. **Plastic Pry Tools**
   These are used to safely open up the device without causing any internal or external damage. Plastic is essential because metal tools can scratch or damage the device's surface.
3. **Suction Cup**
   A suction cup is useful for lifting screens or other tightly secured components from the device.
4. **Heat Gun or Hairdryer**
   Some mobile devices use strong adhesive to hold components together, especially screens. A heat gun or hairdryer is used to soften the adhesive for easier removal.

5. **Tweezers**
   These are used to handle small components inside your device without damaging or dropping them.
6. **SIM Card Ejector Tool**
   Some repairs may involve removing the SIM card tray. A SIM card ejector tool is essential for this purpose.
7. **Multimeter**
   A multimeter is used to check the electrical connections inside the device, such as testing the battery or charging port.
8. **Soldering Iron**
   For more advanced repairs, a soldering iron might be necessary to replace components or repair small circuit boards.
9. **ESD Mat and Wrist Strap**
   Electrostatic discharge (ESD) can damage sensitive internal components. An ESD wrist strap and mat are critical to preventing such damage.

Safety Tips for DIY Mobile Repair

Performing repairs on mobile devices involves handling sensitive electronic parts, and safety is always the top priority. Below are some essential safety tips for DIY mobile device repair:

1. **Power Off Your Device**
   Always ensure that your device is powered off before

you begin any repair. This is critical for avoiding electric shock and protecting internal components.

2. **Work in a Clean, Organized Environment**
   A clean and organized workspace is crucial for ensuring that parts aren't lost or damaged during the repair process. Working in a well-lit area can also help you clearly see tiny parts and screws.

3. **Wear an Anti-Static Wrist Strap**
   When handling internal components, it's important to wear an anti-static wrist strap to prevent electrostatic discharge (ESD) that could damage sensitive parts like the motherboard or battery.

4. **Use the Right Tools for the Job**
   Never force a tool into a tight space. Using the right size screwdriver or pry tool will prevent damage to screws or internal parts.

5. **Handle Parts with Care**
   Some internal parts, like the battery, can be fragile. Handle these components gently, and be mindful of any cables or connectors to avoid breaking them.

6. **Know Your Limits**
   Some repairs, such as replacing a logic board or performing micro-soldering, can be extremely challenging. If you're unsure about a repair, seek professional help.

7. **Use Proper Adhesives**
   When reassembling your device, ensure that you use the proper adhesive strips to secure screens or other

components. Poor adhesives can cause the device to fall apart or not fit properly.

8. **Backup Your Data**
   Before starting any repairs, back up all your important data. Sometimes, repairs can result in data loss, especially if you're replacing internal components like the motherboard.

Understanding the Anatomy of a Mobile Device

To successfully repair mobile devices, it's important to understand how they are built and how the various parts function together. Below is an overview of the essential components inside most mobile devices:

1. **Display (Screen)**
   The screen consists of the **LCD or OLED panel**, which displays images, and the **digitizer**, which detects touch. Screen repairs are one of the most common types of repairs people do.

2. **Battery**
   The battery powers the device and provides the necessary energy for it to function. Over time, the battery can lose its capacity to hold a charge and may need to be replaced.

3. **Motherboard**
   The motherboard, or logic board, is the heart of the device. It houses the central processing unit (CPU),

memory, and other crucial components that allow the device to function.

4. **Charging Port**
   The charging port is where the power cable is connected to the device for charging. Over time, charging ports can become damaged due to repeated plugging in and unplugging.

5. **Speakers and Microphone**
   These components allow the device to produce sound for calls, notifications, and media playback. If they become damaged or clogged, sound issues may arise.

6. **Camera Module**
   Mobile devices often have front and rear cameras. These can malfunction if the lens is scratched or if the internal wiring becomes loose.

7. **Buttons and Switches**
   The power button, volume buttons, and home button (on older devices) are crucial for navigation and operation. These buttons can wear out over time or become unresponsive.

Preparing for Your First Repair

Before you begin your first repair, it's important to prepare yourself mentally and physically. Here are a few steps to take:

1. **Start with Simple Repairs**
   If you're new to mobile repairs, start with something

simple, like replacing a cracked screen or battery. These are straightforward repairs that don't require advanced skills or tools.

2. **Read the Instructions Carefully**
Always read through the repair guides before starting. Watching video tutorials or reading step-by-step instructions will give you a clearer idea of what you need to do.

3. **Take Your Time**
Don't rush through repairs. Taking your time will prevent mistakes and ensure that everything is done properly.

Conclusion

DIY mobile device repair is not only a practical skill but also a rewarding one. It empowers you to extend the life of your device, save money, and learn about the technology that you use every day. As you move through this book, you'll develop the confidence to tackle a variety of common repair tasks, from screen replacements to more advanced issues.

Now that you understand the importance of having the right tools, safety practices, and knowledge, it's time to dive deeper into each repair. In the next chapter, we'll look at how to replace a cracked or damaged screen—one of the most common repairs.

The following is a picture of a Motherboard/ Mainboard:

Chapter 2: Screen Repair

Why Screen Repair Is Important

The screen is one of the most essential parts of a mobile device. It's your interface with the device and is often the first thing people notice. A cracked, shattered, or unresponsive screen can make your phone difficult to use, and in some cases, it may lead to further damage if not repaired promptly. While it might seem daunting, replacing a screen can be a relatively simple task with the right tools and guidance.

Repairing a screen yourself is also a great way to save money. Professional repair services often charge hefty fees, especially for high-end devices like iPhones or Samsung Galaxy phones. This chapter will guide you through the process of replacing a cracked or damaged screen, helping you regain full functionality of your device.

Tools You'll Need for Screen Repair

Before diving into the repair process, it's essential to have the right tools. Here's a list of tools you'll need specifically for screen repair:

1. **Heat Gun or Hairdryer**
   These tools help loosen the adhesive holding the screen to the device.

2. **Suction Cup Tool**
   A suction cup is used to lift the screen from the device's body without causing damage.
3. **Plastic Pry Tools**
   These are used to gently separate the screen from the device after it's been loosened by the heat gun.
4. **Precision Screwdrivers**
   You'll need small screwdrivers to remove screws around the device and screen.
5. **Tweezers**
   Used to remove small parts, like screws or components, safely.
6. **SIM Card Ejector Tool**
   Sometimes, you need to remove the SIM tray to access internal components.
7. **New Replacement Screen**
   Make sure you have the correct replacement screen for your device model.
8. **Adhesive Strips**
   After replacing the screen, you will need fresh adhesive strips to secure the new screen to the device.

Identifying a Damaged Screen

Before proceeding with the repair, you need to determine the extent of the damage to the screen. Here are common types of screen issues:

1. **Cracked or Shattered Screen**
   This is the most common issue. Cracks may be minor

or significant and can sometimes affect the touch functionality of the screen.

2. **Unresponsive Touchscreen**
   If the screen is not responding to touch inputs, but there are no visible cracks, the problem might be with the touchscreen digitizer or the connection between the screen and the motherboard.

3. **Dead Pixels or Display Lines**
   A display with dead pixels (tiny black or discolored spots) or lines running across it may indicate that the screen is faulty.

4. **Ghost Touches**
   If your device is registering touch inputs even when you're not touching the screen, it could be due to internal damage or a faulty digitizer.

Step-by-Step Process to Replace a Screen

Now that you've gathered the tools and identified the issue with your screen, let's begin the step-by-step guide to replacing it.

Step 1: Power Off Your Device

It is crucial to turn off your phone before starting any repair work. This will prevent any accidental electrical shorts and ensure your safety during the repair.

- **Tip**: If you cannot power off the device due to a malfunctioning screen, try holding the power button and volume button simultaneously to force a shutdown.

Step 2: Remove the SIM Card Tray

In many devices, the SIM card tray may be in the way of removing the screen. Use the **SIM card ejector tool** to remove the tray before proceeding with the repair.

- **Tip**: Keep the SIM tray in a safe place to avoid losing it during the repair process.

Step 3: Heat the Edges of the Screen

Using a **heat gun** or **hairdryer**, apply gentle heat to the edges of the screen for about 2-3 minutes. The heat will soften the adhesive holding the screen in place, making it easier to remove.

- **Important**: Make sure not to overheat the device to avoid damaging internal components. Use a low to medium heat setting.

Step 4: Use a Suction Cup Tool to Lift the Screen

Once the device has been heated, attach the **suction cup** to the screen. Gently pull upward to create a small gap between the screen and the device's body.

- **Tip**: If the screen isn't lifting easily, reheat the edges and try again. Be patient—rushing this step can result in damage.

Step 5: Insert a Plastic Pry Tool

After the suction cup has created a small gap, insert a **plastic pry tool** into the space between the screen and the device body. Slowly work your way around the edges to separate the screen from the device.

- **Tip**: Be careful not to force the pry tool, as this could damage the screen or internal components.

Step 6: Disconnect the Battery and Screen Cable

Once the screen is lifted, you will need to disconnect the cables that attach the screen to the motherboard. Use a **precision screwdriver** to remove any screws that secure the screen connector in place. Carefully disconnect the cable using **tweezers**.

- **Tip**: Always disconnect the battery before working with internal components to prevent electrical shock.

Step 7: Remove the Old Screen

After disconnecting the cables, you can fully remove the old screen. Set it aside and clean up any adhesive residue on the device.

- **Tip**: If the old screen is cracked, be cautious and wear gloves to avoid cutting yourself on sharp glass edges.

Step 8: Install the New Screen

Take your new **replacement screen** and align it with the device's body. Reconnect the screen cable to the motherboard and secure it with screws if necessary. Gently press the screen into place.

- **Tip**: Make sure the screen is perfectly aligned before securing it with adhesive.

Step 9: Secure the Screen with Adhesive

Once the screen is in place, use **new adhesive strips** to secure the screen to the device. Press the screen firmly to ensure a strong bond.

Step 10: Reassemble the Device

Reassemble the device by following the steps in reverse order. Insert the SIM card tray back into the device and power it on.

- **Tip**: Make sure all screws are tightened properly and that there are no loose parts before powering on the device.

Step 11: Test the New Screen

Once the device is powered on, test the new screen to make sure it's functioning properly. Check for touch sensitivity, display quality, and any potential dead pixels or lines. If everything is working fine, you've successfully replaced your screen!

Troubleshooting Tips

Sometimes, after replacing a screen, you may encounter issues like unresponsive touch or flickering displays. Here are some troubleshooting tips:

1. **Check Screen Connections**
   If the touchscreen isn't responding, double-check the connectors to ensure they are securely attached.
2. **Test with Another Screen**
   If the new screen doesn't work, there may be an issue with the replacement part. Test the device with another screen to confirm the issue.
3. **Perform a Soft Reset**
   If the device is unresponsive after replacing the screen, try performing a soft reset by holding the power button and volume down button for 10 seconds.

Conclusion

Screen replacement is one of the most common repairs people do on their mobile devices, and with the right tools and steps, it's a task you can complete on your own. By following the step-by-step process in this chapter, you can save money on repairs and give your device a new lease on life.

In the next chapter, we'll discuss how to replace a faulty battery—another essential repair that can restore your phone's functionality.

The following is a picture of a LCD:

Chapter 3: Battery Replacement

Why Battery Replacement Is Important

A mobile device's battery is one of the most critical components. Over time, batteries degrade due to charging cycles, temperature fluctuations, and usage habits. When the battery starts to fail, you may notice:

- **Rapid discharge**: The device loses charge quickly.
- **Slow charging**: It takes longer than usual to charge the device.
- **Inability to hold a charge**: The device shuts down even with some charge remaining.
- **Overheating**: The device gets hot when charging or during heavy use.

If your device exhibits any of these symptoms, it's likely that the battery needs replacing. Performing a DIY battery replacement can save you money and extend the life of your device, especially if you prefer not to go to a repair shop.

Tools You'll Need for Battery Replacement

You'll need the following tools to replace the battery of your mobile device:

1. **Heat Gun or Hairdryer**
   This tool softens the adhesive that holds the battery in place, making removal easier.

2. **Plastic Pry Tools**
   These are used to safely detach the battery from the device without causing damage.

3. **Precision Screwdrivers**
   For removing screws securing the battery compartment or internal covers.

4. **Tweezers**
   These are useful for handling small components, including screws and connectors.

5. **SIM Card Ejector Tool**
   You may need this tool to remove the SIM card tray or internal components that may be blocking access to the battery.

6. **Replacement Battery**
   Be sure to get a battery compatible with your specific device model.

7. **Adhesive Strips**
   After installing the new battery, adhesive strips will secure it in place.

8. **Isopropyl Alcohol and Cleaning Cloth**
   Used for cleaning any residue, dust, or debris left behind during the process.

9. **ESD Mat and Wrist Strap**
   To protect against electrostatic discharge that can damage the device's internal components.

Identifying a Battery Issue

Before you begin the repair process, you need to confirm that the battery is the problem. Here are a few signs that indicate the battery needs to be replaced:

1. **Rapid Battery Drain**
   If your device's battery is draining too quickly, even with light usage, the battery may be nearing the end of its life.
2. **Overheating**
   An overheating battery may not only cause discomfort when holding the device but could also pose a safety risk.
3. **Slow Charging**
   If the device takes too long to charge, or it only charges when the device is powered off, it might be time to replace the battery.
4. **Device Shuts Off Unexpectedly**
   If your device shuts off even when the battery percentage indicates it's still partially charged, this is a clear sign of a failing battery.

Step-by-Step Process for Battery Replacement

Follow the steps below to replace your mobile device's battery:

Step 1: Power Off the Device

Before starting any repair work, always power off your device to avoid electrical issues or damage to internal components.

Step 2: Remove the SIM Card Tray

Using the **SIM card ejector tool**, remove the SIM card tray. This gives you access to the internal components and may also help you better position the device during the repair.

Step 3: Heat the Edges of the Device

If the battery is secured with adhesive, you'll need to soften it. Use a **heat gun** or **hairdryer** to warm up the edges of the device for about 2-3 minutes. This step makes it easier to remove the battery without causing damage.

- **Tip**: Apply heat cautiously. Too much heat can damage the internal components, especially the screen.

Step 4: Pry Open the Device

Using a **plastic pry tool**, gently insert it between the device's casing and the screen. Slowly work your way around the device to separate the body from the screen. If you encounter resistance, reapply heat.

- **Tip**: Take your time to prevent cracking the screen or damaging internal components.

Step 5: Disconnect the Battery Cable

Once the device is open, you will see the battery and its connecting cable. **Disconnect the battery cable** by carefully using your **precision screwdriver** to remove any screws securing the battery connector. Use **tweezers** to gently lift the connector off the motherboard.

- **Important**: Always disconnect the battery first when working with internal components.

Step 6: Remove the Old Battery

Now that the battery is disconnected, it's time to remove it. If the battery is secured with adhesive, use a **plastic pry tool** to gently lift it. If the adhesive is stubborn, reheat the edges of the battery to soften it further.

- **Tip**: Be careful when removing the battery, as applying too much force can damage other internal parts of the device.

Step 7: Install the New Battery

Take your new **replacement battery** and position it inside the device. Reconnect the battery cable to the motherboard and secure it using the precision screwdriver.

- **Tip**: Ensure the new battery is oriented correctly and that all connectors are aligned properly before proceeding.

Step 8: Reassemble the Device

Once the new battery is in place, close the device and reassemble it by reversing the steps. If your device uses adhesive strips to secure the battery, apply new **adhesive strips** to the edges of the battery before sealing the device.

Step 9: Test the New Battery

Once your device is reassembled, power it on and test the new battery. Check to see if the device is charging properly, holding a charge, and that there are no performance issues.

Troubleshooting Tips

If the new battery doesn't seem to work properly, here are some troubleshooting tips:

1. **Check Battery Connection**
   Make sure the battery connector is fully and securely connected to the motherboard.
2. **Test the Charger**
   If the device isn't charging, ensure the charging port is working by testing with a different charger or cable.
3. **Recheck Adhesive**
   If the battery isn't staying in place, make sure the adhesive is applied correctly and securely.
4. **Perform a Soft Reset**
   If the device seems unresponsive, perform a soft reset by

holding down the power button and volume down button for about 10 seconds.

Conclusion

Replacing the battery of your mobile device is an essential repair that can restore the device's functionality and extend its lifespan. By following the step-by-step instructions in this chapter, you can replace a faulty battery on your own, saving time and money in the process.

In the next chapter, we'll cover how to repair or replace a damaged charging port—another vital component in keeping your device operational.

The following is a picture of a Battery:

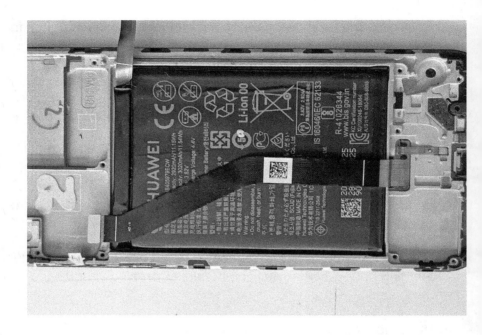

Chapter 4: Charging Port Repair

Why Charging Port Repair Is Important

The charging port is one of the most frequently used components of a mobile device. Over time, it can wear out or become damaged due to constant plugging and unplugging of charging cables. A damaged charging port can cause various issues such as:

- **Device not charging** or charging intermittently.
- **Loose connection** when plugging in the charging cable.

- **Error messages** indicating that the device is not charging properly.
- **Overheating** during charging due to poor contact with the cable.

Repairing or replacing a faulty charging port can restore your device's ability to charge efficiently and ensure it stays connected to accessories. Often, issues with charging ports can be resolved without replacing the port entirely, but in some cases, the port may need to be replaced.

Tools You'll Need for Charging Port Repair

To repair or replace the charging port on your mobile device, you'll need the following tools:

1. **Small Precision Screwdrivers**
   For removing screws securing the device's back cover and the charging port.
2. **Plastic Pry Tools**
   To open the device and separate the charging port area without damaging other components.
3. **Tweezers**
   For handling small parts or components when disassembling the device.
4. **Soldering Iron**
   In cases where the charging port is soldered to the motherboard, a soldering iron may be necessary to remove and replace the port.
5. **Replacement Charging Port**
   If your charging port is damaged beyond repair, you'll need

to get a replacement part. Ensure that it's compatible with your device model.

6. **Isopropyl Alcohol and Cleaning Cloth**
   To clean the charging area and remove any dust, dirt, or debris that could affect charging.

7. **Heat Gun or Hairdryer**
   Used to soften the adhesive securing the charging port in place.

8. **ESD Mat and Wrist Strap**
   Protects against electrostatic discharge that could damage internal components.

Identifying a Charging Port Problem

Before starting the repair, it's important to identify if the charging port is indeed the source of the problem. Here are some common symptoms of a faulty charging port:

1. **Device Not Charging**
   The most obvious sign of a damaged charging port is when your device refuses to charge. This can be due to physical damage or dirt accumulation in the port.

2. **Loose or Flaky Charging**
   If your device charges intermittently or only when the cable is positioned in a certain way, the charging port may be loose or the internal connectors could be worn out.

3. **Error Messages**
   Some devices may display an error message indicating that the charging port is malfunctioning or that it's not recognizing the charging cable.

4. **Physical Damage**
   If the charging port appears bent, cracked, or physically damaged, it may need to be replaced.

Step-by-Step Process for Charging Port Repair

Now let's go through the steps to repair or replace a faulty charging port.

Step 1: Power Off the Device

As with any repair work, the first step is to **power off the device** completely to prevent electrical shorts and ensure your safety during the repair.

Step 2: Remove the SIM Card Tray and Back Cover

Use the **SIM card ejector tool** to remove the SIM card tray if necessary. Afterward, use your **small precision screwdrivers** to remove the screws securing the device's back cover or frame. In some cases, you may need to remove the battery to access the charging port.

Step 3: Inspect the Charging Port for Debris

Before diving into a more complicated repair, inspect the charging port for any debris or dirt. Dust or lint inside the port can prevent a proper connection. Use a **can of compressed air** or a **toothpick** to gently remove any obstructions.

- **Tip**: Never insert anything metal into the port, as this can cause short circuits or permanent damage.

Step 4: Heat the Charging Port Area (If Necessary)

If the charging port is secured with adhesive or is difficult to remove, use a **heat gun** or **hairdryer** to soften the adhesive. Apply heat gently for 1-2 minutes, focusing on the edges around the charging port area.

- **Tip**: Always keep the heat source at a safe distance from the device to avoid damaging internal components.

Step 5: Pry Open the Device

Using a **plastic pry tool**, carefully separate the back cover or the frame from the device to expose the charging port. Take extra care to avoid damaging the surrounding components.

Step 6: Disconnect the Battery (If Necessary)

To ensure safety, it's always best to **disconnect the battery** before working on any internal components. Use a **precision screwdriver** to remove any screws securing the battery and disconnect the cable carefully.

Step 7: Remove the Faulty Charging Port

If the charging port is attached to the device with screws, use your **small precision screwdriver** to remove them. If the port is soldered to the motherboard, use a **soldering iron** to carefully desolder the old charging port.

- **Important**: If you're desoldering, make sure to work in a well-ventilated area and take proper safety precautions.
- **Tip**: Be cautious when using a soldering iron, as it can easily damage surrounding components if not handled correctly.

Step 8: Install the New Charging Port

Take your **replacement charging port** and carefully align it with the connectors on the motherboard. If the new port requires soldering, carefully solder the pins to the motherboard. If it's screwed in, use your precision screwdriver to secure the charging port in place.

- **Tip**: Make sure the new port is aligned properly to ensure a strong connection with the charging cable.

Step 9: Reassemble the Device

Once the new charging port is securely installed, reconnect the battery and reassemble the device. Carefully replace the back cover and tighten the screws.

Step 10: Test the New Charging Port

Power on the device and test the new charging port by plugging in the charging cable. Check if the device charges properly and whether the connection is stable.

- **Tip**: Also test the device with different charging cables to ensure compatibility.

Troubleshooting Tips

If the device isn't charging properly after replacing the charging port, consider the following:

1. **Check the Charging Cable and Adapter**
   Test with different cables and adapters to ensure that the issue isn't with the charger itself.

2. **Inspect the Charging Port Again**
   If the new port isn't working, double-check to ensure that it's connected correctly and that there is no debris or dirt inside.
3. **Check Solder Connections**
   If you used a soldering iron, inspect the solder connections carefully to ensure there are no cold solder joints or loose connections.
4. **Perform a Soft Reset**
   Try performing a soft reset by holding the power button and volume down button for 10 seconds to see if it resolves any system issues.

Conclusion

Repairing or replacing the charging port is a moderately challenging but rewarding repair. By following the step-by-step process in this chapter, you can restore your device's ability to charge properly and avoid costly repairs at a service center.

In the next chapter, we'll discuss how to replace or repair other small components like the camera or buttons, which can help further restore your device's functionality.

The following is a picture of a USB charging port with coax cable:

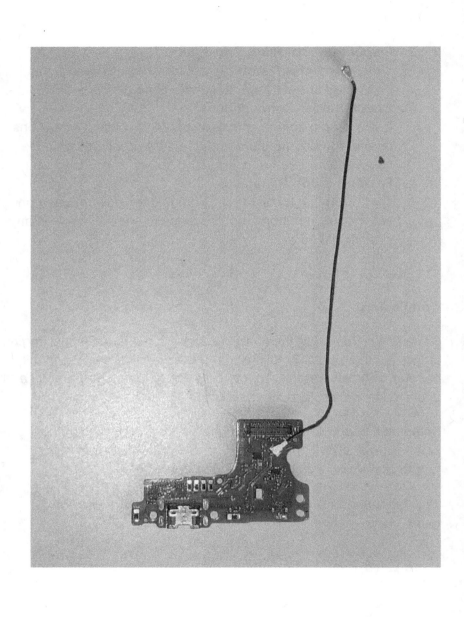

The following is a picture of a USB sub board flex:

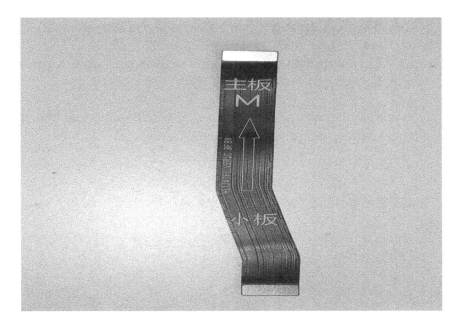

Chapter 5: Button Repair

Why Button Repair Is Important

The buttons on a mobile device play a crucial role in its functionality. Whether it's the power button to turn the device on or off, the volume buttons to adjust sound, or the home button to navigate, a malfunctioning button can severely impact your experience with the device.

Common button issues include:

- **Sticky or unresponsive buttons**: The button doesn't register when pressed, or it feels sluggish.
- **Physical damage**: The button is physically damaged, cracked, or stuck.
- **Complete failure**: The button doesn't work at all, even after pressing.

Repairing or replacing faulty buttons is an affordable and effective way to restore your device's full functionality.

Tools You'll Need for Button Repair

To repair or replace buttons on your mobile device, you'll need the following tools:

1. **Precision Screwdrivers**
   To remove screws securing the device and its components.
2. **Plastic Pry Tools**
   Used for safely opening the device without damaging the internal parts.
3. **Tweezers**
   For handling small components such as button contacts or screws.
4. **Soldering Iron**
   If the button is soldered to the motherboard, a soldering iron will be necessary to remove and replace the button.
5. **Replacement Button**
   Ensure you have the exact replacement part compatible with your device's model.

6. **Isopropyl Alcohol and Cleaning Cloth**
   To clean the button area and remove any dirt or residue that may affect button performance.
7. **ESD Mat and Wrist Strap**
   To protect your device from static electricity while working on it.

Diagnosing Button Issues

Before starting the repair process, it's important to diagnose the issue with your button. Here are some common button problems and their possible causes:

1. **Unresponsive Button**
   If the button doesn't respond to pressing, it could be due to a worn-out switch or a problem with the connection to the motherboard.
2. **Sticky Button**
   If the button feels sticky or doesn't return to its normal position after pressing, debris, dirt, or sticky residue may be causing the issue.
3. **Button Not Making Contact**
   Sometimes the button may not make proper contact with the underlying switch or motherboard, resulting in it not functioning.
4. **Physical Damage**
   Cracks, dents, or breakages in the button or surrounding area can affect the functionality of the button.

Step-by-Step Process for Button Repair

Follow these steps to repair or replace the buttons on your mobile device.

Step 1: Power Off the Device

Before performing any repair work, make sure your device is powered off completely to avoid electrical damage and ensure your safety.

Step 2: Remove the SIM Card Tray

Use the **SIM card ejector tool** to remove the SIM card tray. This will allow you to access internal components and may also give you additional room to work during the repair process.

Step 3: Remove the Back Cover or Frame

Use a **precision screwdriver** to remove the screws securing the back cover or the frame of the device. In some cases, you may also need to remove the battery or other components to access the button assembly.

- **Tip**: Keep track of the screws, as some may be different sizes and need to go back in specific locations.

Step 4: Inspect the Button Area for Damage or Debris

Once the device is open, inspect the area around the button. Check for physical damage, such as cracks or broken parts. Also, look for dirt, dust, or sticky residue around the button that might be causing it to malfunction.

- **Tip**: Use **isopropyl alcohol** and a **cleaning cloth** to gently clean around the button area. This can help remove dirt or grime that may be affecting the button's performance.

Step 5: Remove the Faulty Button

Depending on your device, the button may be secured with screws or adhesive. If the button is secured with screws, use the **precision screwdriver** to remove them. If the button is held in place with adhesive, use a **plastic pry tool** to gently lift it.

If the button is physically damaged, you may need to replace it with a new one. Be careful not to damage any surrounding components while removing the faulty button.

Step 6: Install the New Button

Once the old button is removed, carefully install the **new button** by aligning it with the device's button mechanism. If the button is secured with screws, tighten them with a screwdriver. If it uses adhesive, carefully press the button into place, making sure it is positioned correctly.

- **Tip**: Make sure the button clicks into place and makes proper contact with the internal switch, which is responsible for registering button presses.

Step 7: Reassemble the Device

After installing the new button, reassemble the device by reversing the steps you took to disassemble it. Replace the back cover or frame and secure it with screws. If you had to remove the battery or any internal components, reattach them carefully.

Step 8: Test the Button

Once the device is reassembled, power it on and test the new button to ensure it's working properly. Press the button several times to check if it responds and feels normal. If it's a home button, test its functionality by navigating through the device.

- **Tip**: If the button is still unresponsive or feels sticky, you may need to open the device again and check the alignment or the connection to the motherboard.

Troubleshooting Tips

If the button doesn't seem to work properly after replacement, consider the following troubleshooting steps:

1. **Check the Button Alignment**
   Make sure the new button is aligned correctly with the

internal switch or motherboard. Misalignment can prevent proper contact.

2. **Inspect the Button Mechanism**
   Ensure the internal mechanism (the switch or connector) is not damaged or obstructed by dirt or debris.
3. **Check for Residual Adhesive**
   If you used adhesive, ensure there is no leftover adhesive that might be interfering with the button's movement.
4. **Perform a Soft Reset**
   If the device is unresponsive after button replacement, perform a soft reset by holding the power button and volume down button for 10 seconds.

Conclusion

Repairing or replacing buttons on your mobile device is a relatively simple repair that can greatly improve your experience. By following the steps in this chapter, you can troubleshoot and fix problems with unresponsive, sticky, or damaged buttons without the need for professional help.

In the next chapter, we'll cover how to repair or replace the screen of your mobile device—one of the most common (and often most expensive) repairs.

Chapter 6: Screen Repair

Why Screen Repair Is Important

The screen is the most important part of your mobile device, as it serves as both the display and the primary interface for interacting with the device. A broken, cracked, or unresponsive screen can render your phone nearly unusable, affecting:

- **Touchscreen functionality**: If the touchscreen doesn't register your taps or swipes, it becomes hard to operate the device.
- **Display issues**: Cracks, dead pixels, or discoloration can make the screen difficult to read or look at.
- **Aesthetic damage**: Cracked or shattered glass can make your device look unsightly.

Repairing or replacing a damaged screen can restore both the function and the appearance of your device, saving you money compared to replacing the entire device.

Tools You'll Need for Screen Repair

To repair or replace the screen on your mobile device, you'll need the following tools:

1. **Precision Screwdrivers**
   For removing screws that secure the device's frame and screen components.

2. **Plastic Pry Tools**
   To carefully separate the screen from the body without damaging the internal components or the screen itself.
3. **Suction Cup Tool**
   Used to lift the screen away from the device's frame without cracking it.
4. **Heat Gun or Hairdryer**
   To soften any adhesive that may be holding the screen in place, making it easier to remove.
5. **Replacement Screen**
   Ensure that you have a compatible replacement screen for your device model. This could include the digitizer, LCD, and glass, depending on the repair.
6. **Isopropyl Alcohol and Cleaning Cloth**
   To clean the area around the screen and remove adhesive residue or fingerprints.
7. **Tweezers**
   For handling small screws and delicate parts when removing or installing the screen.
8. **ESD Mat and Wrist Strap**
   To protect your device from electrostatic discharge during the repair process.

Diagnosing Screen Problems

Before jumping into the repair, it's important to understand what kind of screen issue you're dealing with. Here are some common screen problems:

1. **Cracked or Shattered Glass**
   A cracked or shattered screen is often the result of a drop or

impact. Although the screen might still display images, the broken glass can be dangerous and affect the device's usability.

2. **Unresponsive Touchscreen**
   If your screen no longer responds to touch or registers input intermittently, it could be due to a problem with the digitizer (the touch-sensitive layer of the screen).

3. **Display Issues**
   If the screen shows vertical lines, dead pixels, discoloration, or a black screen, the LCD (Liquid Crystal Display) might be damaged. This can also occur if the screen has been exposed to water or extreme pressure.

4. **Backlight Issues**
   If the screen is very dim or doesn't light up at all, even though the device is powered on, it could be a backlight issue, which typically means the LCD or backlight component needs to be replaced.

Step-by-Step Process for Screen Repair

Follow these steps to repair or replace your mobile device's screen.

Step 1: Power Off the Device

Before starting the repair, **power off the device** completely to avoid any electrical damage or accidental input while working.

Step 2: Remove the Back Cover and Battery

Use a **precision screwdriver** to remove the screws securing the device's back cover. If necessary, also remove the battery and any internal components that are blocking access to the screen.

- **Tip**: Be careful not to damage the internal cables or components when removing the back cover.

Step 3: Apply Heat to Soften the Adhesive

In most devices, the screen is glued to the frame with a strong adhesive. Use a **heat gun** or **hairdryer** to warm up the edges of the screen for 1-2 minutes. This will soften the adhesive, making it easier to remove the screen without cracking it.

- **Tip**: Keep the heat source at a safe distance (around 2-3 inches) to prevent overheating and damaging other parts of the device.

Step 4: Lift the Screen Using the Suction Cup Tool

Place the **suction cup tool** near the edge of the screen and gently pull to create a small gap between the screen and the device's frame. Once there is enough space, use a **plastic pry tool** to carefully slide between the screen and the frame to loosen the adhesive.

- **Tip**: Work slowly and carefully to avoid damaging the screen or the internal components.

Step 5: Disconnect the Screen's Internal Connectors

Once the screen is loosened, carefully remove it from the device. You'll likely encounter several **internal connectors** (such as ribbon cables) that attach the screen to the motherboard. Use **tweezers** or a **plastic pry tool** to disconnect these connectors.

- **Tip**: Make sure to remember the placement of each connector so you can reconnect them properly during reassembly.

Step 6: Remove the Old Screen

Once all connectors are disconnected, carefully remove the damaged screen. If it's cracked or shattered, handle it with extra caution to avoid injury from broken glass.

- **Tip**: If the screen is still attached by strong adhesive, you may need to apply more heat to soften it further.

Step 7: Clean the Screen Area

Before installing the new screen, clean the **frame area** using **isopropyl alcohol** and a soft cloth to remove any adhesive residue, dust, or fingerprints.

Step 8: Install the New Screen

Place the new screen into position, ensuring that it aligns with the connectors and the device's frame. Gently reconnect all the internal connectors to the motherboard. If the new screen uses adhesive, press it into place firmly.

- **Tip**: Take your time to ensure that all connectors are securely attached.

Step 9: Reassemble the Device

Once the new screen is installed, carefully reassemble the device. Replace the battery and back cover, and secure them with screws.

Step 10: Test the New Screen

Power on the device and test the new screen. Check that the touchscreen is responsive and that the display is clear, without any dead pixels or discoloration.

- **Tip**: Also check for touch sensitivity and test for proper display brightness and color reproduction.

Troubleshooting Tips

If the screen doesn't seem to be functioning properly after replacement, consider the following troubleshooting steps:

1. **Check the Connectors**
   Make sure all connectors are properly reattached.
   Sometimes, a loose connector can cause the screen to
   malfunction.
2. **Inspect for Debris**
   Ensure there is no dust or debris between the screen and
   the device, as this can affect the touch sensitivity or display.
3. **Reapply Adhesive**
   If the screen doesn't sit properly, you may need to use new
   adhesive or double-sided tape to secure the screen.
4. **Perform a Soft Reset**
   Try restarting the device by holding down the power button
   and volume down button for 10 seconds.

Conclusion

Screen repairs, though delicate, are one of the most common and
rewarding DIY mobile repairs. By following the steps outlined in this
chapter, you can restore a damaged or malfunctioning screen and
bring your device back to life. Always handle the screen with care
to avoid cracks and injuries, and take your time to ensure
everything is properly connected.

In the next chapter, we'll cover advanced repairs, such as replacing
internal components like the motherboard or camera.

Chapter 7: Advanced Repairs

Why Advanced Repairs Are Important

While basic repairs like screen and button replacement are more common, there are times when issues with your mobile device go deeper into the internal components. The **motherboard**, **camera**, and **other advanced components** are critical for the overall function of the device. Problems with these parts can lead to issues such as:

- **System crashes or freezing**: Often related to motherboard failure.
- **Camera malfunctions**: Such as blurry images or the inability to open the camera app.
- **Battery issues**: Internal components like charging ports or the motherboard can affect battery performance.

Repairing or replacing these components can restore your device's functionality, though these repairs are typically more intricate and require additional precautions.

Tools You'll Need for Advanced Repairs

When performing advanced repairs, you'll need tools that allow for precise work on delicate internal components. These tools include:

1. **Precision Screwdrivers**
   To remove the small screws securing internal parts like the motherboard and camera.

2. **Plastic Pry Tools**
   For safely detaching components without causing damage.
3. **Soldering Iron**
   If the motherboard or camera module is soldered onto the device, a soldering iron is required for careful removal and reinstallation.
4. **Tweezers**
   For handling small components, especially when working with delicate motherboard or camera parts.
5. **ESD Mat and Wrist Strap**
   To prevent static damage to the internal components.
6. **Multimeter**
   Useful for diagnosing issues on the motherboard or checking for continuity and power in different components.
7. **Replacement Parts**
   These include a new motherboard, camera module, or any other internal component that needs replacing.

Diagnosing Advanced Issues

Before you start the repair, you need to diagnose the specific issue with your device. Here are some signs that indicate the need for advanced repairs:

1. **Motherboard Issues**
   If your device is freezing, restarting, or not responding properly, the motherboard might be the culprit. Damage to the motherboard could also cause the phone to not turn on, or not recognize certain components like the camera or charging port.
   Common symptoms of motherboard failure include:

- Frequent crashes or system failures
- Overheating
- No response when trying to power on the device

2. **Camera Issues**

   If the camera app crashes, the camera produces blurry images, or the camera app doesn't open at all, it could be due to a malfunctioning camera module or related connections.

   Symptoms include:
   - Blurry or out-of-focus images
   - Camera app not opening or crashing
   - The camera not being detected by the device

3. **Charging Port Issues**

   If your device isn't charging properly, it could be due to a faulty charging port or motherboard. This can happen if the port becomes loose or damaged after prolonged use.

Step-by-Step Process for Advanced Repairs

Below are the steps for repairing or replacing the motherboard and camera module of your mobile device.

Replacing the Motherboard

Step 1: Power Off the Device

Before starting, **power off the device** completely to avoid any electrical damage.

Step 2: Disassemble the Device

Remove the back cover, SIM card tray, and battery from the device. Depending on the device model, you might need to remove screws and other components, such as the display or mid-frame, to access the motherboard.

- **Tip**: Keep track of all screws and parts you remove during the disassembly process.

Step 3: Disconnect All Internal Connectors

Once the device is open, use a **plastic pry tool** and **tweezers** to disconnect all connectors attached to the motherboard. This may include the display connector, camera module, battery, and other components.

Step 4: Remove the Faulty Motherboard

Carefully remove the screws securing the motherboard and gently lift it out of the device. Be cautious not to damage any surrounding components or ribbon cables.

- **Tip**: Make a note of how the motherboard is oriented in the device for reinstallation.

Step 5: Install the New Motherboard

Place the new motherboard in position and secure it with screws. Reconnect all internal connectors, including the display, camera, and battery.

- **Tip**: Double-check that all connectors are properly seated and aligned.

Step 6: Reassemble the Device

Once the motherboard is in place and connected, reassemble the device by reversing the steps you took during disassembly. Replace the back cover, SIM card tray, and battery.

Step 7: Test the Device

Power on the device and test all features to ensure the motherboard replacement was successful. Check for any performance issues, such as slow processing or unresponsive apps.

Replacing the Camera Module

Step 1: Power Off the Device

As with the motherboard replacement, ensure the device is powered off before starting.

Step 2: Disassemble the Device

Remove the back cover and any components that might block access to the camera, such as the battery or mid-frame.

- **Tip**: Keep track of all parts and screws.

Step 3: Disconnect the Camera Module

Locate the camera module, which is often connected to the motherboard via a ribbon cable. Use tweezers or a plastic pry tool to carefully disconnect it.

Step 4: Remove the Faulty Camera Module

Unscrew the screws securing the camera module in place. Carefully lift it out of the device.

Step 5: Install the New Camera Module

Place the new camera module into position, ensuring it is aligned with the connectors. Reattach the screws and reconnect the camera's ribbon cable to the motherboard.

Step 6: Reassemble the Device

Reassemble the device by reversing the steps. Make sure all connectors are reattached, and the device is properly closed.

Step 7: Test the Camera

Power on the device and test the new camera. Open the camera app and take some photos to check if the camera is functioning correctly.

Troubleshooting Tips

1. **Motherboard Repair**
   If the device doesn't power on after replacing the motherboard, double-check all internal connectors and ensure the motherboard is securely seated. If the device still doesn't respond, the new motherboard may need further diagnosis or a second replacement.
2. **Camera Repair**
   If the camera is still malfunctioning after replacement, ensure the camera module is securely connected to the

motherboard. If the problem persists, the issue might be with the software or an issue deeper on the motherboard.

3. **Test Everything Thoroughly**
   When working with advanced repairs, it's essential to test each component thoroughly before reassembling the device. This ensures that any issues can be identified early and prevents the need to reopen the device multiple times.

Conclusion

Advanced repairs, such as replacing the motherboard or camera, require patience and precision but can be highly rewarding. These repairs can restore your device to full functionality, making it as good as new. While these repairs are more challenging than basic fixes like screen replacement, with the right tools and approach, you can confidently tackle these more complex issues.

In the next chapter, we'll discuss **Battery Replacement** and the importance of keeping your mobile device's battery in good condition.

The following is a picture of a camera:

Chapter 8: Battery Replacement

Why Battery Replacement Is Important

Batteries degrade naturally over time, especially with heavy use. As the battery ages, you may notice the following issues:

- **Shorter Battery Life**: Your device might need to be charged more frequently throughout the day.
- **Charging Problems**: The device may fail to charge or charge slowly, indicating a problem with the battery or charging circuit.
- **Overheating**: A faulty battery can cause your device to overheat, which could lead to other internal damage.
- **Unexpected Shutdowns**: The device may shut off unexpectedly, even if the battery level appears to be sufficient.

If you're experiencing any of these issues, it might be time for a battery replacement.

Tools You'll Need for Battery Replacement

Replacing a battery in your mobile device requires specific tools. Here's what you'll need:

1. **Precision Screwdrivers**
   To remove the screws securing the back cover and internal components.

2. **Plastic Pry Tools**
   To carefully open the device without damaging it.
3. **Suction Cup Tool**
   To help remove the screen or back cover without cracking or damaging it.
4. **Spudger Tool**
   A plastic tool used for disconnecting battery connectors and removing adhesive.
5. **Replacement Battery**
   Ensure you have a compatible replacement battery designed for your device model.
6. **Tweezers**
   For handling small screws and delicate components.
7. **Isopropyl Alcohol and Cleaning Cloth**
   For cleaning the internal parts of the device once it's open.
8. **ESD Mat and Wrist Strap**
   To prevent damage from static electricity during the repair process.

Diagnosing Battery Problems

Before you begin replacing the battery, it's important to ensure that the problem lies with the battery and not other components, such as the charging port or motherboard. Here are a few common signs that indicate battery issues:

1. **Device Drains Battery Quickly**:
   If the battery life is significantly shorter than usual, even after updating apps or the operating system, it's likely a battery issue.

2. **Battery Percentage Inaccuracy**:
   If the battery percentage suddenly drops (e.g., from 50% to 10%) or the device powers off unexpectedly, this may indicate a failing battery.
3. **Charging Problems**:
   If your device fails to charge properly, either not charging at all or charging slowly, this could also be a sign that the battery needs replacement.
4. **Overheating**:
   An overheated device, especially when charging, can indicate a damaged battery. Batteries that overheat can become a safety risk.

Step-by-Step Process for Battery Replacement

Follow these steps to replace the battery in your mobile device:

Step 1: Power Off the Device

The first step in any repair is always to **power off** the device completely to avoid electrical damage and potential injury.

Step 2: Remove the Back Cover or Screen

If your device has a removable back cover, simply use a **plastic pry tool** to lift it off. If the screen is glued to the frame, you'll need to use a **suction cup tool** to gently separate the screen from the body. You may need to use a heat gun to soften the adhesive if it's particularly strong.

- **Tip**: Be very careful when removing the screen as the display can be easily cracked or damaged.

Step 3: Disconnect the Battery

Once the device is open, locate the battery. It will be connected to the motherboard via a connector. Use a **plastic pry tool** or **spudger** to carefully disconnect the battery's ribbon cable.

- **Tip**: Always disconnect the battery before working with other internal components to avoid short circuits.

Step 4: Remove the Old Battery

In many devices, the battery is secured with strong adhesive. To remove the battery, use a **plastic pry tool** or a **spudger** to gently lift the battery out of its compartment. Be careful not to puncture the battery during removal.

- **Tip**: If the battery is difficult to remove, you can apply a small amount of heat with a **hairdryer** or **heat gun** to soften the adhesive.

Step 5: Install the New Battery

Place the new battery into the compartment, ensuring it's correctly aligned. Carefully reconnect the battery's ribbon cable to the motherboard. Press the battery into place to ensure it adheres properly.

- **Tip**: Some batteries come with adhesive pre-applied, but you can use double-sided tape or adhesive strips to secure it if needed.

Step 6: Reassemble the Device

After installing the new battery, reassemble the device by reversing the disassembly steps. If you removed the back cover or screen, carefully reattach it and secure it with screws if necessary.

- **Tip**: Make sure everything is properly aligned, and no cables are pinched during reassembly.

Step 7: Test the New Battery

Power on the device and check the battery's performance. Test charging, battery life, and the device's general performance. Make sure the battery is holding charge and charging correctly.

- **Tip**: It may take a few charge cycles for the new battery to reach its full capacity.

Troubleshooting Tips

1. **Device Won't Turn On After Battery Replacement**
   If your device doesn't power on after replacing the battery, check the battery connections to ensure they are secure. You might also want to perform a **soft reset** by holding the power button and volume down button for 10 seconds.
2. **Battery Not Charging**
   If the device isn't charging after the battery replacement, double-check that the charging port is clean and free of debris. If the charging port looks fine, it could be an issue with the new battery or the charging circuit on the motherboard.
3. **Device Overheats**
   If your device is overheating after replacing the battery, it could be caused by an incorrectly installed battery, short circuit, or poor battery quality. Double-check the connections and ensure the battery is seated properly.

Conclusion

Replacing the battery in your mobile device is a relatively straightforward task, but it's essential to handle the components carefully to avoid damage. A new battery can breathe new life into your device, restoring long battery life and performance. Be sure to use a high-quality replacement battery and test the device thoroughly once the repair is complete.

In the next chapter, we'll explore how to **maintain your device** after a repair and ensure that it continues to run smoothly.

The following is a picture of a Back cover with fingerprint sensor and flex:

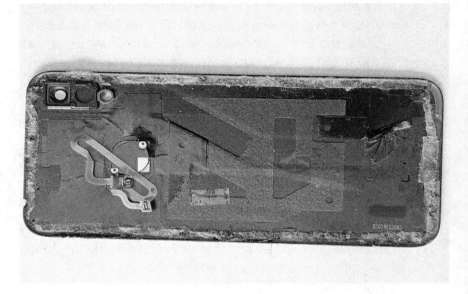

Chapter 9: Device Maintenance

Why Device Maintenance Is Important

Maintaining your mobile device after repairs ensures that it continues to operate smoothly and efficiently. Regular maintenance not only helps prevent future problems but also extends the life of your device. Proper maintenance includes both **hardware care** (cleaning, battery care, etc.) and **software upkeep** (updates, system optimization, etc.).

Here are the key areas to focus on:

1. **Regular Cleaning**
   Keeping your device clean is essential to prevent dust, dirt, and debris from causing issues, especially after internal repairs. Dirt accumulation can damage components such as the charging port, screen, and buttons.
2. **Software Updates**
   Updating your device's software ensures you have the latest features, bug fixes, and security patches. It also helps maintain the overall stability of the system.
3. **Battery Care**
   Proper battery maintenance can extend its lifespan and improve performance. This includes not overcharging, using the device within an appropriate temperature range, and avoiding extreme discharges.
4. **Hardware Protection**
   Using protective cases, screen protectors, and keeping the device away from excessive heat, moisture, and rough handling can help preserve the hardware after a repair.

Essential Maintenance Practices

Here are the steps you can take to maintain your mobile device after repairs:

1. Regular Cleaning

Why It's Important
Dust, dirt, and oils from your hands can accumulate inside your device and cause damage. These particles can obstruct charging ports, buttons, and touchscreens, leading to performance issues.

How to Clean Your Device
Follow these cleaning tips to maintain your device:

- **Screen and Body**:
  Use a **microfiber cloth** to wipe the screen and body of the device. If needed, dampen the cloth with a small amount of water or isopropyl alcohol (preferably 70% or higher) to remove stubborn fingerprints or dirt. Avoid using paper towels, which can scratch the screen.
- **Charging Port**:
  Use a **soft brush** or a can of compressed air to clean out the charging port. Be gentle to avoid damaging the port. You can also use a toothpick to carefully remove any lint or dirt stuck inside, but be cautious not to damage the connectors.
- **Speakers and Microphone**:
  Gently clean the speaker and microphone areas with a dry,

soft brush. Compressed air can also help remove dirt and debris from these areas.

2. Update Software Regularly

Why It's Important
Software updates fix bugs, introduce new features, and improve the security of your device. Outdated software can cause instability, slow down your device, and expose it to security vulnerabilities.

How to Update Software
To keep your device up to date:

- **Check for Updates**:
  Go to **Settings** > **Software Update** or **About Device** > **System Update** (depending on your device). If an update is available, download and install it.
- **Enable Automatic Updates**:
  Set your device to automatically download and install updates when they become available. This ensures that you always have the latest version without needing to remember to check manually.

3. Maintain Battery Health

Why It's Important
A properly maintained battery lasts longer and performs better, which is crucial for the overall performance of your device.

Tips for Battery Maintenance

- **Avoid Overcharging**:
  Although modern devices are designed to stop charging once the battery reaches 100%, keeping it plugged in for long periods can still reduce battery lifespan. Try to unplug the device once it reaches 100% if possible.
- **Don't Let the Battery Fully Discharge**:
  Avoid letting your battery completely drain to 0%. Charging it when it's between 20% and 80% helps maintain battery health.
- **Charge in the Right Temperature**:
  Charging your device in extreme temperatures (either very hot or very cold) can damage the battery. Make sure the device is in a well-ventilated area during charging, and avoid leaving it in a hot car or direct sunlight.
- **Use Original Chargers**:
  Always use the charger that came with the device or a certified third-party charger. Non-certified chargers can damage the battery or cause charging issues.

4. Hardware Protection

Why It's Important
Protecting your device physically helps preserve the newly repaired components, such as the screen and back cover, and prevents damage from drops, scratches, and dust.

How to Protect Your Device

- **Use a Case**:
  A protective case can absorb impact and prevent scratches. Choose a case that fits your device snugly without obstructing ports or buttons. Opt for a case that has raised edges to protect the screen.
- **Screen Protector**:
  Apply a **screen protector** to safeguard the screen from scratches and minor impacts. Tempered glass protectors offer better protection against cracks compared to plastic ones.
- **Avoid Exposure to Extreme Conditions**:
  Keep your device away from extreme heat or cold. Avoid exposing it to moisture, which can cause internal damage, especially after internal repairs.
- **Keep It Clean**:
  Regularly clean your device (as discussed earlier) to remove dust and grime that can accumulate in hard-to-reach areas, like ports and crevices.

5. Back Up Your Data Regularly

Why It's Important
Backing up your data ensures that you don't lose important files in case of a failure. A good backup system allows you to restore your data if the device gets damaged again or if you need to perform a factory reset.

How to Back Up Your Data

- **Cloud Services**:
  Use **cloud storage services** like Google Drive, Apple iCloud, or Dropbox to back up important files, photos, and videos.
- **External Storage**:
  For larger files or a full device backup, consider using an external hard drive or a computer.
- **Automatic Backups**:
  Set your device to automatically back up your data to the cloud whenever it's connected to Wi-Fi. This will ensure your data is always safe.

6. Perform System Optimization

Why It's Important
Optimizing your device's performance ensures it runs smoothly and efficiently, even after multiple repairs.

How to Optimize Your Device

- **Clear Cache**:
  Clear the app cache regularly to free up space and improve app performance. You can do this by going to **Settings > Storage > Cached Data**.
- **Uninstall Unused Apps**:
  Remove apps that you no longer use to free up space and improve system performance.
- **Factory Reset (If Necessary)**:
  If your device is still sluggish after maintenance, you can

perform a **factory reset**. This will erase all data and restore the device to its original factory settings, so be sure to back up your data first.

Conclusion

Maintaining your device after repairs is key to ensuring its longevity and continued performance. Regular cleaning, software updates, battery care, and hardware protection will keep your device in excellent condition for years to come. By following these simple maintenance practices, you can avoid future issues and get the most out of your mobile device.

In the next chapter, we'll discuss how to **troubleshoot common issues** that may arise even after performing repairs. Let me know when you're ready to continue!

Chapter 10: Troubleshooting Common Issues

Why Troubleshooting Is Important

No device, no matter how well-maintained, is immune to occasional issues. Some problems may arise after repairs, while others could be unrelated issues that need to be addressed. Being able to diagnose and fix common problems will save you time and money and help keep your device functioning smoothly.

In this chapter, we will cover troubleshooting for the following common issues:

- **Device Won't Turn On**
- **Touchscreen Not Responding**
- **Charging Issues**
- **Overheating**
- **Poor Battery Performance**
- **Audio or Speaker Issues**
- **Wi-Fi and Bluetooth Connectivity Problems**
- **Software Glitches**

1. Device Won't Turn On

Possible Causes:

- **Battery issues**: A faulty or improperly installed battery may prevent your device from turning on.
- **Loose connections**: Internal connectors, such as the battery ribbon cable or screen connectors, may not be properly seated.
- **Power button problems**: The power button may not be functioning correctly after a repair.

Troubleshooting Steps:

1. **Check the Battery**: Ensure the battery is properly connected to the motherboard. If you've recently replaced the battery, verify that the battery ribbon cable is securely attached.

2. **Force Restart**: Try a hard reset or force restart by holding down the power button and volume down button (or the specific combination for your device) for 10 seconds to see if the device powers on.
3. **Check for Physical Damage**: Inspect the power button to make sure it is functioning correctly. If it appears stuck or unresponsive, it may need to be repaired or replaced.

2. Touchscreen Not Responding

Possible Causes:

- **Display issues**: After screen replacement, the screen may not be properly connected to the motherboard.
- **Software glitches**: Sometimes, software issues can make the touchscreen unresponsive.
- **Dirty screen**: Oil, dirt, or moisture on the screen can cause unresponsiveness.

Troubleshooting Steps:

1. **Clean the Screen**: Use a microfiber cloth to gently clean the touchscreen, removing any dust or oils.
2. **Check the Screen Connection**: If the issue started after a screen replacement, ensure the screen's ribbon cable is securely connected to the motherboard.
3. **Restart the Device**: Perform a soft restart by holding down the power button and selecting "Restart" from the options.
4. **Check for Software Updates**: Sometimes, software glitches can affect the touchscreen functionality. Go to **Settings** > **Software Update** to check for updates.

3. Charging Issues

Possible Causes:

- **Charging port issues**: Dirt or damage to the charging port may prevent the device from charging properly.
- **Faulty charging cable or adapter**: Using a damaged or incompatible charging cable or adapter can lead to charging problems.
- **Battery problems**: A damaged battery may fail to charge or charge erratically.

Troubleshooting Steps:

1. **Inspect the Charging Port**: Check for any debris or dirt in the charging port. Use compressed air or a brush to clean the port gently.
2. **Test the Charging Cable**: Try using a different charging cable and adapter to see if the problem lies with the charger.
3. **Check the Battery**: If the charging port and cable seem fine, the battery may be the issue. If you recently replaced the battery, make sure it is properly installed.
4. **Try Wireless Charging**: If your device supports wireless charging, test it to see if the charging issue is related to the physical charging port.

4. Overheating

Possible Causes:

- **Heavy usage**: Running resource-intensive apps, like games or video streaming, can cause the device to overheat.

- **Battery issues**: A damaged or improperly installed battery can cause excessive heat.
- **Poor ventilation**: Keeping your device in a hot environment or using it while it's charging can also lead to overheating.

Troubleshooting Steps:

1. **Stop Using Intensive Apps**: Close any apps that are consuming a lot of resources, such as games or video streaming apps.
2. **Check the Battery**: Ensure the battery is properly installed. Overheating can sometimes be a sign of a malfunctioning battery.
3. **Allow the Device to Cool**: Turn off the device and let it cool down for a few minutes before using it again.
4. **Check the Device's Environment**: Avoid using your device in extreme temperatures or while charging in direct sunlight.

5. Poor Battery Performance

Possible Causes:

- **Battery degradation**: Older batteries lose their ability to hold charge and discharge quickly.
- **Power-hungry apps**: Certain apps or settings can drain the battery rapidly.
- **Improper calibration**: The battery percentage may be inaccurate if the device has not been calibrated properly.

Troubleshooting Steps:

1. **Check Battery Usage**: Go to **Settings** > **Battery** and check the battery usage breakdown. Identify apps that are consuming too much power and close or uninstall them if necessary.
2. **Calibrate the Battery**: If the battery percentage is fluctuating, let the battery discharge completely and then recharge it fully to 100%.
3. **Replace the Battery**: If the battery is old and no longer holding a charge properly, it may be time for a replacement.

6. Audio or Speaker Issues

Possible Causes:

- **Speaker damage**: The speaker could be physically damaged after a drop or repair.
- **Software problems**: Audio issues can sometimes be caused by software glitches or settings problems.
- **Loose connections**: If the audio cable or connector isn't properly attached, the sound may be distorted or absent.

Troubleshooting Steps:

1. **Check the Volume and Mute Settings**: Ensure the volume is turned up and the device is not on mute.
2. **Test with Headphones**: Plug in a pair of headphones to determine if the issue lies with the speakers or the audio software.

3. **Inspect the Speaker**: If you recently replaced the screen or the back cover, check that the speaker is properly connected and seated. If the speaker is damaged, you may need to replace it.
4. **Restart the Device**: A simple restart can sometimes resolve audio software glitches.

7. Wi-Fi and Bluetooth Connectivity Problems

Possible Causes:

- **Software glitches**: Sometimes, software bugs can interfere with Wi-Fi or Bluetooth connections.
- **Network issues**: Problems with your home Wi-Fi network or Bluetooth device pairing may also cause connectivity issues.
- **Damaged antenna**: If the Wi-Fi or Bluetooth antenna is damaged during repairs, connectivity will be affected.

Troubleshooting Steps:

1. **Restart the Device**: A restart can resolve temporary connectivity issues caused by software glitches.
2. **Toggle Wi-Fi/Bluetooth**: Turn Wi-Fi or Bluetooth off and on again to reset the connection.
3. **Forget and Reconnect to Wi-Fi/Bluetooth**: Go to **Settings > Wi-Fi/Bluetooth**, forget the network or device, and reconnect.
4. **Check for Software Updates**: Make sure your device's software is up-to-date to avoid any connectivity bugs.

5. **Inspect Antennas**: If you've recently replaced the screen or other components, check the antenna connections.

8. Software Glitches

Possible Causes:

- **Corrupted files**: Sometimes, apps or files can become corrupted and cause the device to slow down or crash.
- **Outdated software**: An outdated operating system can lead to bugs and glitches.

Troubleshooting Steps:

1. **Reboot the Device**: Sometimes, a simple reboot can resolve minor software issues.
2. **Clear Cache**: Go to **Settings** > **Storage** > **Cached Data** and clear the cache to free up space and improve performance.
3. **Factory Reset**: If the problem persists, you may want to perform a factory reset. Be sure to back up your data before doing this.

Conclusion

Troubleshooting common issues is an essential skill for anyone performing DIY repairs on their mobile device. By understanding the potential causes and knowing how to diagnose and fix problems, you can ensure that your device continues to function properly after repairs. Regular maintenance and careful attention to issues will also prevent future problems.

In the next chapter, we'll discuss **advanced repairs** and how to tackle more complex issues like motherboard repairs, camera fixes, and other in-depth repairs. Let me know when you're ready to continue!

The following is a picture of a top ear speaker with proximity sensor board:

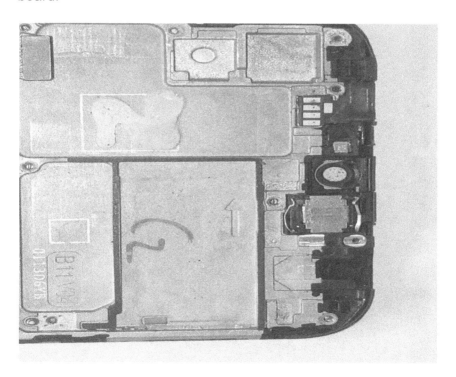

The following is a picture of a Loud speaker:

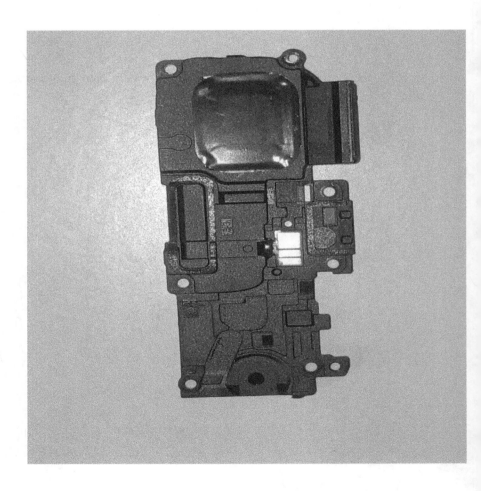

The following is a picture of a vibrator:

Chapter 11: Advanced Repairs

Why Advanced Repairs Are Necessary

While basic repairs, such as screen replacements or battery swaps, are fairly straightforward, more advanced repairs are necessary when dealing with critical components like the motherboard or camera. These repairs require more skill, patience, and often specialized tools.

Performing advanced repairs allows you to breathe new life into a device that might otherwise be deemed irreparable. However, it's important to understand that these repairs can be more time-consuming and risky, especially if you're new to mobile device repair. Properly diagnosing the issue and having the right tools are crucial for success.

In this chapter, we'll cover:

- **Motherboard Repairs**
- **Camera Repairs**
- **Replacing Charging IC (Integrated Circuit)**
- **Replacing the Audio IC**
- **Reflowing/Reballing Solder for Circuit Boards**
- **Screen Digitizer Repair**

1. Motherboard Repairs

Why It's Important: The motherboard is the heart of the device. If the motherboard is damaged, it can lead to issues like the device not turning on, being unresponsive, or malfunctioning. Sometimes, these issues can be traced back to damaged components on the motherboard, like capacitors, resistors, or other vital parts.

Common Problems with Motherboards:

- **Physical Damage**: Cracks or broken traces from a drop or internal damage.
- **Water Damage**: Moisture exposure can cause short circuits or corrosion on the motherboard.
- **Component Failure**: Chips or components failing after an impact or due to age.

How to Repair:

1. **Identify the Issue**:
    - Visually inspect the motherboard for any obvious signs of damage, such as cracked traces, burnt components, or discolored areas.
    - Use a multimeter to check for continuity and voltage readings, helping pinpoint the damaged area.
2. **Remove the Damaged Component**:
    - Use a **soldering iron** and **solder wick** to remove any damaged or faulty components carefully.
    - For delicate components, use **desoldering pumps** to remove excess solder.
3. **Replace the Component**:
    - Once the faulty component is removed, place a new one in the same position.
    - Solder the new component in place and make sure it's securely attached.

4. **Test the Device**:
   - ○ After replacing the component, test the device to ensure the repair has been successful. Check for power and functionality.

Important Tools Needed:

- Soldering Iron with fine tip
- Multimeter
- Solder Wick
- Desoldering Pump
- Microscope (optional for precise inspection)

2. Camera Repairs

Why It's Important: The camera is one of the most used components on modern devices. If your camera isn't working correctly, you may experience blurry pictures, non-functional autofocus, or no image at all.

Common Problems with Cameras:

- **Cracked lens**: Physical damage to the camera lens after a drop or impact.
- **Camera not recognized**: Sometimes, a disconnected or faulty cable can prevent the device from recognizing the camera.
- **Malfunctioning autofocus**: Dirt, debris, or damage to the camera module can cause autofocus failure.

How to Repair:

1. **Diagnose the Issue**:
   - Check if the issue is related to the lens or the camera module.
   - Open the camera app and see if there's an error message or if it's not launching.
2. **Replace the Camera Module**:
   - Power down the device and remove the back cover.
   - Disconnect the battery and carefully detach the camera module from the motherboard.
   - Replace the camera module with a new one, ensuring the connector is securely attached.
3. **Test the Camera**:
   - After the repair, power the device back on and test the camera functionality. Check for picture clarity, focusing ability, and video recording.

Important Tools Needed:

- Pry tools
- Soldering iron (for connecting the camera module if necessary)
- Replacement camera module
- Anti-static wristband

3. Replacing the Charging IC (Integrated Circuit)

Why It's Important: The charging IC controls how your device receives and distributes power during charging. If the charging IC is faulty, your device might not charge correctly, could overheat, or may not recognize charging at all.

Common Issues:

- **Charging stops working**: The device fails to charge when plugged in.
- **Overheating during charging**: Excessive heat is generated when charging, which could be a sign of a faulty IC.
- **Inconsistent charging**: The device charges intermittently, sometimes charging but then stopping.

How to Repair:

1. **Diagnose the IC**:
   - If charging issues persist after replacing cables and adapters, inspect the charging IC for visible damage or signs of overheating.
2. **Remove the Old IC**:
   - Use your soldering iron to carefully desolder the charging IC from the motherboard.
   - Make sure to remove any residual solder with a desoldering pump or wick.
3. **Install the New Charging IC**:
   - Place the new charging IC in the correct position and solder it into place. Be sure the connections are secure.
4. **Test the Charging**:
   - After replacing the IC, test the charging port and verify that the device is charging properly.

Important Tools Needed:

- Soldering Iron
- Desoldering Pump/Wick
- Multimeter
- Replacement Charging IC

4. Replacing the Audio IC

Why It's Important: The audio IC controls all audio functions, including speaker output, microphone input, and headphone jack signals. If the audio IC is damaged, you may experience issues with sound quality, no sound, or microphone failure.

How to Repair:

1. **Diagnose the Issue**:
   - Test if all audio functions (speakers, headphones, microphone) are affected or if only specific parts are malfunctioning.
2. **Locate the Audio IC**:
   - Use a schematic or repair manual for your specific device to locate the audio IC on the motherboard.
3. **Desolder the Faulty IC**:
   - Using a fine-tipped soldering iron, carefully desolder the audio IC and remove it.
4. **Replace the Audio IC**:
   - Install the new IC in the same position and solder it securely in place.
5. **Test the Audio**:

- Once the new IC is installed, test the device's audio functions, including speakers and microphone.

Important Tools Needed:

- Soldering Iron
- Multimeter
- Replacement Audio IC

5. Reflowing/Reballing Solder for Circuit Boards

Why It's Important: Reflowing and reballing are techniques used to repair damaged solder joints or to replace damaged components that have become detached. This is often used when a device has issues with connectivity or if the motherboard has been damaged.

How to Perform:

1. **Reflowing:**
   - Apply heat to the solder joints using a heat gun or reflow station. This will melt the solder and allow the components to reconnect.
2. **Reballing:**
   - If the solder balls on the IC are damaged or missing, you can replace them by placing new solder balls and heating them to reflow.

Important Tools Needed:

- Heat Gun/Reflow Station
- Solder Balls

- Soldering Iron
- Microscope (for precision)

6. Screen Digitizer Repair

Why It's Important: If the touch functionality of your screen is not working, or the screen is cracked but the display still functions, the issue could be with the **digitizer**. The digitizer is responsible for detecting touch input.

How to Repair:

1. **Remove the Screen**:
   - Carefully remove the screen from the device, ensuring no damage is done to the LCD panel.
2. **Detach the Digitizer**:
   - The digitizer is usually glued to the screen. Use a heat gun or suction cup to loosen the glue and carefully peel off the digitizer.
3. **Install the New Digitizer**:
   - Attach the new digitizer to the screen and reconnect the ribbon cable to the motherboard.
4. **Test the Touchscreen**:
   - Test the screen's touch functionality to ensure it responds correctly.

Important Tools Needed:

- Suction Cup
- Heat Gun
- Pry Tools

- Replacement Digitizer

Conclusion

Advanced repairs involve dealing with the most critical and sensitive parts of a mobile device, such as the motherboard and essential ICs. These repairs require a high level of skill, precision, and the right tools. While these types of repairs are more complicated and carry more risk, with practice, you can master these skills and become an expert in mobile device repairs.

In the next chapter, we will cover **professional repair services** and when it's best to seek out expert help. Let me know when you're ready to move forward!

Chapter 12: Professional Repair Services

Why Consider Professional Repair Services?

As much as DIY repairs are satisfying, certain repairs may be too complicated, risky, or time-consuming for an individual to handle effectively. Additionally, some repairs require specialized tools and knowledge that are often unavailable to the average consumer. In these cases, professional repair services can be invaluable.

Here are some reasons why you might need professional help:

- **Complex Repairs**: Some repairs, such as motherboard repairs or reballing ICs, are complex and require expert knowledge and equipment.
- **Time Constraints**: If you don't have the time or patience to learn and perform the repair, a professional can save you the hassle.
- **Risk of Further Damage**: Incorrect repairs can often lead to more significant damage. A professional repair service will help avoid these risks.
- **Warranty Concerns**: In some cases, DIY repairs can void warranties, while professional repairs can be covered by service guarantees.

When Should You Seek Professional Help?

Here are some specific scenarios in which you should consider taking your device to a professional repair service:

1. **Motherboard Damage**:
   - If your device is experiencing issues that seem related to the motherboard, such as a failure to power on or random reboots, this is not a repair most DIY technicians can fix without the right equipment and expertise.
   - **Warning Signs**: Burnt areas on the motherboard, visible cracks, or issues with internal components like charging ICs or CPU.
   - **Why Professional Repair is Needed**: Repairing a motherboard involves delicate work such as reballing, reflowing solder, or replacing chips, which requires specialized tools and knowledge to do properly.
2. **Water Damage**:
   - Water damage is one of the most common causes of failure in mobile devices. It can lead to rust, corrosion, and damage to critical components. Often, water damage requires deep cleaning, board inspection, and component replacement, which is best handled by professionals.
   - **Warning Signs**: Device not powering on after contact with water, visible corrosion, or unusual behavior even after drying.
   - **Why Professional Repair is Needed**: Professionals have specialized equipment, such as ultrasonic cleaners, to remove corrosion and clean the motherboard without causing further damage.
3. **Screen Issues with No Display**:
   - If your device has a cracked or damaged screen and replacing the digitizer or LCD does not solve the

issue, the problem could be deeper, such as with the GPU (graphics processing unit) or motherboard.
- ○ **Warning Signs**: Flickering screen, no display after screen replacement, distorted visuals.
- ○ **Why Professional Repair is Needed**: Professionals have diagnostic tools like oscilloscopes to test the GPU and determine if there is a deeper issue beyond the screen.

4. **Battery Issues Beyond Replacement**:
   - ○ While battery replacement is a common DIY repair, sometimes battery problems are caused by the charging IC or internal power circuitry. If replacing the battery doesn't fix the issue, or if the battery is draining rapidly or overheating, it may be a more complex problem.
   - ○ **Warning Signs**: Device not charging properly even after battery replacement, overheating when charging.
   - ○ **Why Professional Repair is Needed**: Professional technicians can diagnose power-related issues at the circuit level and replace damaged components like charging ICs.

5. **Audio, Wi-Fi, and Bluetooth Failures**:
   - ○ If the audio, Wi-Fi, or Bluetooth functionality is not working despite troubleshooting, the issue might lie with the internal components or ICs. Replacing these components requires skill and precision.
   - ○ **Warning Signs**: No sound from speakers or microphone, inability to connect to Wi-Fi or Bluetooth, low reception quality.
   - ○ **Why Professional Repair is Needed**: Professionals can test and replace faulty audio ICs, antennas, or

chips and use their diagnostic tools to ensure everything is working correctly.

How to Find a Reputable Repair Service

When choosing a professional repair service, it's important to research and find a trustworthy and qualified technician or repair center. Here's how you can go about it:

1. **Look for Reviews and Testimonials**:
   - Search for customer reviews and ratings online. Websites like Google Reviews, Yelp, and Trustpilot can give you an idea of the repair center's reliability and customer satisfaction.
   - **Tip**: Look for repair shops with positive reviews specifically related to the types of repairs you need.
2. **Check for Certifications**:
   - A reputable technician should have relevant certifications or experience working with mobile devices, particularly with the type of repair you need. Certifications like Apple Certified Technician, Samsung Certified Repairer, or similar are good indicators of quality.
   - **Tip**: Ask if the technician is certified or has experience working with your specific device model.
3. **Warranty and Guarantees**:
   - Professional repair services should offer a warranty or guarantee on their work. This gives you peace of mind in case the issue is not fully resolved after repair or if the part fails again shortly after being replaced.

- ○ **Tip**: Always ask about the warranty or guarantee before agreeing to the repair.

4. **Get an Estimate**:
   - ○ Always request a detailed estimate that breaks down the cost of labor, parts, and any potential extra charges. A reputable service provider will give you a transparent quote.
   - ○ **Tip**: If the estimate seems unusually low, be cautious, as it may indicate that the service is cutting corners.

5. **Consider the Turnaround Time**:
   - ○ Depending on the complexity of the repair, the turnaround time may vary. Make sure the repair shop gives you an estimated time for when your device will be ready for pickup or delivery.
   - ○ **Tip**: Check if the repair service offers expedited services if you need your device back urgently.

What to Expect from a Professional Repair

Once you've selected a reputable professional repair service, here's what you can expect during the repair process:

1. **Initial Diagnosis**:
   - ○ The technician will begin by diagnosing the problem with your device. This may involve a visual inspection, running diagnostics, or testing specific components to isolate the issue.

2. **Repair Process**:
   - ○ After the diagnosis, the technician will discuss the repair options and provide you with a time frame for

completing the repair. In most cases, you will need to leave the device with the technician for a few hours or days, depending on the severity of the issue.

3. **Replacement of Faulty Parts**:
   o The technician will replace any faulty or damaged components, such as the motherboard, camera, battery, or screen. They will use high-quality replacement parts that are either original (OEM) or compatible with your device.

4. **Testing**:
   o After the repair, the technician will test your device to ensure everything is functioning correctly. They will check the display, charging port, audio, connectivity, and other functions to confirm the repair has been successful.

5. **Return of Device**:
   o Once the repair is complete, the technician will return your device to you. You should test the device thoroughly to ensure it's working as expected. If there are any remaining issues, don't hesitate to inform the technician.

Cost of Professional Repairs

The cost of professional repairs can vary widely depending on the type of repair, the device model, and whether the repair involves replacing internal components or the motherboard. Here are some general price ranges:

- **Screen Replacement**: $50 - $250

- **Battery Replacement**: $40 - $150
- **Motherboard Repair**: $100 - $500
- **Camera Module Replacement**: $30 - $200
- **Audio IC or Charging IC Replacement**: $40 - $150
- **Water Damage Repair**: $50 - $300

Tip: Always get a written estimate and ensure that parts are included in the total cost.

Conclusion

While DIY repairs can save you money and help you learn valuable skills, there are situations where professional repair services are necessary. When dealing with complex issues such as motherboard damage, water damage, or component-level repairs, seeking professional help ensures the repair is done properly and reduces the risk of further damage. Always take the time to research repair services, ask for recommendations, and ensure you're working with qualified technicians.

In the next chapter, we will cover **maintaining your device for long-term use**, focusing on habits and practices to keep your device running smoothly for years. Let me know when you're ready to continue!

Chapter 13: Maintaining Your Device for Long-Term Use

Why Device Maintenance is Important

Just like any other technology, mobile devices require maintenance to function optimally over time. Whether it's keeping the screen clean, managing software updates, or protecting the internal components, regular maintenance can prolong the life of your device and prevent costly repairs down the road.

Neglecting maintenance can lead to performance slowdowns, battery issues, and physical damage. Luckily, keeping your device in good condition is not difficult and can be done with just a few simple steps. In this chapter, we'll cover:

- **Basic Cleaning and Care**
- **Battery Care and Management**
- **Software and System Updates**
- **Protecting Your Device**
- **Avoiding Common Pitfalls**
- **Regular Inspections and Troubleshooting**

1. Basic Cleaning and Care

Why It's Important: Keeping your device clean is crucial not just for aesthetics, but also for its longevity. Dust, dirt, and oils from your skin can accumulate on your device, particularly around ports, the screen, and the camera. Over time, this buildup can lead to performance issues or even hardware damage.

Cleaning Tips:

- **Screen and Exterior**:
    - Use a soft, lint-free microfiber cloth to wipe down the screen and back of the device.
    - For tougher smudges, lightly dampen the cloth with water or a 70% isopropyl alcohol solution. Avoid harsh chemicals that can damage the screen coating.
    - Regularly clean the ports and buttons with a soft brush or compressed air to prevent dust buildup.
- **Charging Port**:
    - Use a toothpick or a small brush to gently clean the charging port. Be cautious not to damage the pins inside the port.
    - If you see dirt or lint inside, compressed air can help clear it out.
- **Cameras and Lenses**:
    - Clean the camera lens with a soft cloth to avoid blurry photos caused by fingerprints or dust. Always use a clean microfiber cloth designed for lenses to avoid scratches.

Tips:

- Clean your device at least once a week.
- Avoid using abrasive materials, as these can scratch the device.
- Don't use cleaning agents like bleach or ammonia.

2. Battery Care and Management

Why It's Important: The battery is one of the most crucial components of a mobile device. Over time, it will degrade, and if not managed properly, it may wear out prematurely. However, with proper battery care, you can extend its lifespan and maintain optimal performance.

Battery Care Tips:

- **Avoid Extreme Temperatures**:
    - Exposure to excessive heat or cold can damage the battery and reduce its lifespan. Keep your device out of direct sunlight and avoid charging it in hot environments.
    - If possible, store your device in a cool, dry place.
- **Charging Practices**:
    - Avoid letting your battery drain completely to 0% regularly. Lithium-ion batteries, which are commonly used in mobile devices, last longer when they are charged between 20% and 80%.
    - Avoid overcharging your device. Unplug it once it reaches 100%, or use a smart charger that prevents overcharging.
    - If you plan not to use the device for an extended period, charge the battery to around 50% before storing it. This helps maintain the health of the battery.
- **Battery Calibration**:
    - Occasionally, let the battery run down to 0% and then charge it back to 100% in a single cycle. This

helps recalibrate the battery's internal software, providing more accurate battery readings.

- **Use Power Saving Mode**:
  - Most devices come with a built-in power-saving mode. Activating this feature will reduce unnecessary background activity and increase battery life.

Battery Replacement:

- Battery life will inevitably degrade over time, and if you notice that your device is not holding a charge as well as it used to, consider replacing the battery. Some devices allow for easy battery replacement, while others may require professional assistance.

3. Software and System Updates

Why It's Important: Keeping your device's software up to date is essential for security, performance, and functionality. Software updates often include bug fixes, performance improvements, and new features, ensuring that your device remains secure and runs efficiently.

Update Tips:

- **Enable Automatic Updates**:
  - Most mobile devices have an option to automatically download and install software updates. Enable this feature to ensure that your device stays up to date without manual intervention.

- **Check for Updates Regularly**:
  - If you don't have automatic updates enabled, check your device's settings every couple of weeks to see if new updates are available.
- **Backup Your Data**:
  - Before performing major software updates, it's always a good idea to back up your data to ensure you don't lose anything important in case the update causes issues.
- **Clean Up Your Device**:
  - When updating your software, take the opportunity to clear out unnecessary files or apps. This will free up space, reduce clutter, and improve your device's performance.
  - Use the built-in tools on your device to clear cache files and uninstall apps that you no longer use.

4. Protecting Your Device

Why It's Important: Protecting your device from physical damage is as important as keeping it clean. Investing in a few protective accessories can help prevent costly repairs and keep your device looking new.

Protection Tips:

- **Use a Case**:
  - A good-quality protective case can shield your device from drops, scratches, and other physical damage. Look for cases that offer adequate corner protection and are made of durable materials.

- Consider a case with a built-in screen protector to guard the display against scratches and cracks.
- **Use a Screen Protector**:
    - A screen protector is an affordable and effective way to prevent scratches and minor cracks. There are various types, including tempered glass and film protectors, each offering different levels of protection.
- **Avoid Water Exposure**:
    - Unless your device is rated for water resistance, avoid using it in wet conditions. If your device does get wet, dry it off immediately and allow it to air-dry before turning it on.

5. Avoiding Common Pitfalls

Why It's Important: Knowing what to avoid can prevent unnecessary damage and help you maintain your device's functionality. Here are some common mistakes and how to avoid them:

- **Overcharging**:
    - Leaving your device plugged in overnight regularly can slowly degrade the battery over time. This is particularly true for older devices that don't have optimized charging circuits.
- **Unnecessary Apps and Bloatware**:
    - Overloading your device with unnecessary apps and files can lead to performance issues and increased storage consumption. Remove unused apps, and be selective about what you install.

- **Ignoring Overheating**:
  - ○ If your device starts to overheat, it's essential to address the issue immediately. Overheating can damage internal components and significantly shorten the device's lifespan.
  - ○ Remove any case or cover while charging to allow for heat dissipation.

6. Regular Inspections and Troubleshooting

Why It's Important: Regularly inspecting your device and troubleshooting minor issues can prevent bigger problems later on. If you catch problems early, you can often address them before they require expensive repairs.

Inspection Tips:

- **Check for Software Errors**:
  - ○ Regularly run diagnostics to check for software glitches or errors. This can often be done within your device's settings, and it will help improve overall performance.
- **Inspect Ports and Buttons**:
  - ○ Regularly inspect the charging port, headphone jack, and other ports for any signs of wear or dirt buildup.
- **Monitor Battery Health**:
  - ○ Keep an eye on your battery health through the settings or an app that provides detailed battery statistics. If you notice a significant decline in battery capacity, it may be time to replace the battery.

Conclusion

Maintaining your mobile device is essential for ensuring its longevity and optimal performance. By following simple habits such as keeping it clean, charging properly, updating software, and using protective accessories, you can significantly extend the life of your device and avoid unnecessary repairs. Regular inspections and addressing small issues early can save you time and money in the long run.

In the next chapter, we'll provide a final recap of everything you've learned and offer tips on how to continue growing your repair skills. Let me know when you're ready for the final wrap-up!

Conclusion: Mastering Mobile Device Repairs and Maintenance

Congratulations on completing the guide to repairing and maintaining mobile devices! By now, you have gained a wealth of knowledge, ranging from diagnosing common issues to performing DIY repairs and understanding when to seek professional help. You've also learned how to maintain your device for long-term use, ensuring it continues to perform optimally.

In this final chapter, we will recap the key points from each chapter, offer some final tips for honing your repair skills, and provide resources for further learning.

Key Takeaways from the Book

1. **Understanding Your Device**:
   - Familiarity with your mobile device's components, such as the screen, battery, motherboard, and internal ICs, is crucial for effective repairs.
   - Regular inspections and knowledge of how to troubleshoot problems can save time and money.
2. **DIY Repair Techniques**:
   - Performing repairs on your device, from screen replacements to battery swaps, can be rewarding and cost-effective.
   - Having the right tools, like a heat gun, soldering iron, and precision screwdriver set, is essential for safe and effective repairs.
3. **Internal and External Inspections**:
   - External inspections focus on visible damage like cracks or dents, while internal inspections involve checking for damaged or malfunctioning internal components like the motherboard and chips.
   - Regular checks can help detect problems early, preventing major issues from escalating.
4. **Safety and Precautions**:
   - Always prioritize safety when handling electronic devices. Use the right tools, work in a safe environment, and follow the correct procedures to prevent personal injury or device damage.
   - Safety protocols include working in a well-lit space, grounding yourself to prevent static discharge, and ensuring the device is powered off before repairs.

5. **Tools and Equipment**:
   - Basic tools like screwdrivers, pry tools, tweezers, and suction cups are necessary for most repairs.
   - Specialized tools, such as a soldering iron, hot air station, and multimeter, are required for more complex repairs like motherboard rework or IC replacement.
6. **Professional Repair Services**:
   - Know when to seek help from professionals. For repairs that are beyond your expertise, such as motherboard reballing or intricate component-level repairs, consider taking your device to a certified technician.
   - A professional repair service can provide warranty-backed repairs and offer expertise that minimizes the risk of causing further damage.
7. **Maintaining Your Device**:
   - Regular maintenance, including cleaning the screen, charging port, and camera lenses, helps prevent buildup that can affect performance.
   - Battery management, software updates, and using protective cases and screen protectors are all crucial to preserving the health of your device.
   - Regularly check for software updates and clear out unused apps to ensure your device runs efficiently.

Final Tips for Improving Your Repair Skills

1. **Practice Makes Perfect**:

- Start with simple repairs, such as replacing a cracked screen or battery, before moving on to more complex tasks like motherboard repairs or reflowing solder.
- Don't be afraid to make mistakes—learning from them is a part of the process.

2. **Stay Updated on Trends**:
   - Mobile technology is constantly evolving. New devices, parts, and repair techniques emerge regularly. Stay informed by reading repair blogs, watching tutorials, and joining online forums dedicated to mobile repair.

3. **Document Your Work**:
   - Keep a repair journal or document your repairs with photos and notes. This will help you learn from each repair and track which methods work best for different issues.
   - Sharing your experience in online communities can also help others and open up opportunities for feedback.

4. **Join Repair Communities**:
   - Participate in online forums and social media groups that focus on mobile device repairs. These communities can offer valuable advice, troubleshooting tips, and support.
   - Some popular repair communities include Reddit's r/mobilerepair, iFixit, and YouTube channels dedicated to repair tutorials.

5. **Expand Your Skill Set**:
   - Consider learning advanced techniques like soldering and micro-soldering. These skills will open

up opportunities for more complex repairs, such as motherboard and chip-level work.
- ○ Enroll in repair workshops or online courses to improve your technical knowledge and gain hands-on experience.

Further Resources

Here are some additional resources to help you continue your repair journey:

- **iFixit**: Offers a wide range of repair guides, tools, and parts for mobile devices and other electronics. A great starting point for beginners and experts alike. iFixit
- **Online Courses**:
  - ○ **Udemy**: There are various courses related to mobile repair, ranging from basic repairs to advanced soldering techniques.
  - ○ **Skillshare**: Offers courses on electronic repair, including mobile devices and computers.
- **Mobile Repair Blogs**:
  - ○ **Phone Repair Tools**: Offers advice on mobile device repairs and a list of tools required for DIY repairs.
  - ○ **Tech Repairs**: A blog offering tips and how-tos on common mobile device repairs and troubleshooting.

Conclusion

By following the steps outlined in this guide, you now have the skills to diagnose, repair, and maintain your mobile device. Whether you're fixing a cracked screen, replacing a faulty battery, or tackling more complex motherboard issues, you've gained the confidence to approach repairs with the right tools and techniques.

Remember, regular maintenance and knowing when to seek professional help are key to prolonging the life of your device. Don't hesitate to continue practicing, learning, and experimenting to refine your skills. Repairing mobile devices can be a fulfilling and rewarding skill that not only saves money but also allows you to keep your devices in great condition for years to come.

Final Words

You now have the knowledge and tools to repair, maintain, and troubleshoot your mobile devices. Whether you're doing it for personal satisfaction or considering a career in repair services, mobile device repair is a valuable skill that continues to grow in demand. Stay curious, keep learning, and you'll be able to handle any mobile device repair challenge that comes your way!

Good luck, and happy repairing!